China Clipper

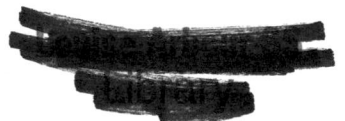

Also by Richard Brignall in the Lorimer Recordbooks series:

Big League Dreams: Baseball Hall of Fame's first African-Canadian, Fergie Jenkins

Big Train: The legendary ironman of sport, Lionel Conacher

Fearless: The story of George Chuvalo, Canada's greatest boxer

Forever Champions: The enduring legacy of the record-setting Edm̶o̶n̶t̶o̶n̶ ̶G̶r̶a̶d̶s̶

Small Town Glory: The story of the Kenora Thistles' remarkable quest for the Stanley Cup (with John Danakas)

China Clipper

Pro football's first Chinese-Canadian player, Normie Kwong

Richard Brignall

James Lorimer & Company Ltd., Publishers
Toronto

James Lorimer & Company Ltd., Publishers acknowledges the support of the
Ontario Arts Council. We acknowledge the financial support of the Government
of Canada through the Canada Book Fund for our publishing activities. We
acknowledge the support of the Canada Council for the Arts for our publishing
program. We acknowledge the Government of Ontario through the Ontario
Media Development Corporation's Ontario Book Initiative.

The Canada Council | Le Conseil des Arts
for the Arts | du Canada

ONTARIO ARTS COUNCIL
CONSEIL DES ARTS DE L'ONTARIO

Cover design: Meredith Bangay

Library and Archives Canada Cataloguing in Publication

Brignall, Richard
        China Clipper : pro-football's first Chinese-Canadian player, Normie
Kwong / Richard Brignall.

(Recordbooks)
Issued also in an electronic format.
ISBN 978-1-55277-528-8 (bound).--ISBN 978-1-55277-527-1 (pbk.)

        1. Kwong, Norman, 1929- --Juvenile literature. 2. Chinese
Canadian football players--Biography--Juvenile literature. I. Title. II. Series:
Record books

GV939.K86B75 2010	j796.335092	C2010-904072-4

James Lorimer & Company Ltd., Publishers
317 Adelaide Street West,
Suite #1002
Toronto, ON, Canada
M5V 1P9
www.lorimer.ca

Distributed by:
Orca Book Publishers
P.O. Box 468
Custer, WA USA
98240-0468

Printed and bound in Canada.
Manufactured by Printcrafters in Winnipeg, Manitoba, Canada in August 2010.
Job # 27287

I would like to dedicate this book to my co-workers and friends during my time at the Manitoban — the student newspaper at the University of Manitoba. It was the most influential time in my life and an experience I will never forget. And, without that experience, I would not have written this book. Thank you all.

Contents

Prologue 9

1   The Struggle to be Canadian 14

2   The Unlikely Neighbourhood Star 21

3   The Benchwarmer 27

4   Calgary's Big Game 35

5   First-String Starter 41

6   Injury Scare 50

7   Battle of Alberta 56

8   Edmonton's Time to Shine 63

9   A Football Revolution 73

10 A Battle to the End 79

11 The Western Underdogs 86

12 Kwong's Last Stand 98

13 Not a Fluke 107

14 The City of Champions 115

15 Endgame 121

Epilogue 131

Football Basics 137

Glossary 141

Acknowledgements 145

About the Author 147

Photo Credits 148

Index 149

Prologue

The modern Grey Cup game was born in 1948. The actual game was played the same way as before. But that year the Canadian football championship got a little more exciting. It all centred on the Calgary Stampeders' first appearance in the big game.

Before 1948, western teams that challenged eastern teams for the Cup were accompanied by few fans. They watched the game and then went back home. They were just faces in the crowd.

The 1948 Grey Cup became a party. Stampeders fans were at the centre of it all. Two hundred and fifty Calgarians boarded a special train headed for Toronto. Easterners thought their rivals didn't have much to celebrate. The Calgarians were just excited their hometown heroes finally made it to the championship.

Calgary Alderman Don McKay said it was time to inject some colour into the event. He wanted to take Calgary's greatest celebration, the Calgary Stampede, to the eastern city. Since 1912 the Stampede had brought broncobusters, calf ropers, and bull riders from all over North America to Calgary.

The Stampeders' fans donned their favourite clothes. The women wore red silk blouses and white ten-gallon hats. The men dressed in full cowboy gear, including chaps and spurs. They also loaded horses and chuckwagons onto the train.

On the day before the Grey Cup game, that special train pulled into Toronto's Union Station. The party in Toronto began as the westerners exited the train whooping and hollering. The group paraded to the Royal York hotel. Men played accordions while couples broke into square dances along the city street. One man carried a lasso, which he used to rope people as they walked by him. People ran out of restaurants and office buildings to watch the strange show.

A reporter asked one westerner, "I suppose it's ridiculous to ask who's going to win Saturday?"

There was a great cowboy yell. Then his hand slapped down on the reporter's back. The westerner replied, "It certainly is son, it certainly is."

Calgary fans planned the first Grey Cup parade through the city streets. Toronto Mayor Hiram McCallum was caught up in the spirit of the moment. He accepted a challenge to ride a horse down Bay Street the morning of the game.

The parade started in front of the Royal York. It followed Bay Street with Mayor McCallum riding along on a horse. On the steps of Toronto's City Hall they stopped and enjoyed a pancake breakfast. Then the parade of horses, chuckwagons, and 250 brightly dressed people headed for the football stadium. The Grey Cup, East-West clash, started at 1:45 p.m.

The Stampeders football players entered the big game quietly. They were not part of the celebration put on by their fellow Calgarians. They didn't want anything to take away their focus on the game.

Those Calgary fans transformed the Grey Cup into an important event. People now come from across the country to be part of the celebration. The parade and pancake breakfast are rituals that continue each year.

The 1948 Grey Cup game was important for another reason. For one Stampeders player that game was more than a western party. It was the end of a history-making season. Nineteen-year-old rookie Normie Kwong became the first Chinese-Canadian professional football player that year. He was more than an oddity who was quickly forgotten. He became one of the greatest players in league history.

Normie always saw himself as just a football player. But he played for more than glory on the football field. He represented the hopes and dreams of Chinese Canadians across Canada.

1 The Struggle to be Canadian

At first, the Chinese were welcomed into Canada. They were encouraged to immigrate because Canada needed workers to build the national railway. Starting in 1880, 17,000 Chinese, mostly men, came to Canada to work. They helped build the difficult and dangerous sections of the railway in British Columbia. Seven hundred Chinese workers died working on that 563-kilometre (350-mile) stretch of railway. They were paid only half the wage of white workers.

Once the railway was finished five years later, there was no more need for cheap labour. The message the Chinese were given by the Canadian government was clear. Chinese people weren't welcome in Canada anymore.

The Canadian government went to great lengths to keep Chinese immigrants out of the country. In 1885 the government introduced the Act to Restrict and Regulate Chinese Immigrants to Canada. It required Chinese people entering Canada to pay a fee to the government. This was called a Head Tax.

At first Chinese people entering the country had to pay $50. This was a large amount at that time, but they still came to Canada. They would do anything to escape the poverty in their homeland. Whole families paid the tax. The government thought too many Chinese were coming over, so they raised the Head Tax to $100 in 1902. People still came, so one year later it was raised to $500. This was two years' wages in China. Now, instead of whole families coming, just men came to Canada. They left their wives and children behind. The lucky ones eventually had enough money to bring over their families.

White citizens treated the Chinese even worse than the government did. They did more than just call them names. They attacked Chinese workers and hurt them. Some burned down their homes and businesses. They wanted to keep Canada "white."

To further their battle against the Chinese, the Canadian government passed The Chinese Immigrant Act in 1923. It was better known as the Chinese Exclusion Act. It stopped all Chinese immigrants from entering Canada. Many wives and children in China were unable to join their husbands and fathers in Canada.

Under this new law, all Chinese people already in Canada had to register with the government. Even those people born in Canada still had to sign up. On July 1, 1923 all Chinese Canadians were no longer legal Canadians.

Normie Kwong was born into this Canada on October 24, 1929.

Normie's father, Charles Lim Kwong, had immigrated to Canada from China in 1907. He paid the Head Tax. He went to work on the railway. Normie's mother, Lily Lee, came to Canada with her family in 1912. Charles and Lily's parents arranged for them to be married.

As Chinese Canadians they were barred from owning land and property and from doing certain jobs. Norm's parents found hardship and discrimination in British Columbia. It was a segregated society where white and Chinese citizens lived

Chinese Canadians in traditional dress for a 1935 parade in Edmonton.

by different rules. Many restaurants, for example, would not serve Chinese people.

Charles and Lily Kwong moved to Calgary, Alberta. Discrimination against them lessened when they left British Columbia. Charles opened his own business. He owned and operated the Riverside Cash and Carry Store.

The Kwongs had six children. The fifth

child was Lim Kwong Yew. His Canadian name was Norman Lim Kwong. Normie and his siblings were lucky to have both parents in Canada. Many Chinese children grew up separated from one parent.

As a child, Normie learned first-hand what it was like to be different. One time, he wanted to go into the wading pool at the park. His sister stopped him. Normie wondered why until she told him Chinese people were not allowed in the pool.

In 1947, the Chinese Exclusion Act was reversed. It was found to be against the United Nations Charter of Human Rights that Canada signed after the Second World War. Chinese Canadians were given the right to vote in federal elections. It wasn't until 1949 that they could vote in British Columbia provincial elections. For the first time, Chinese Canadians were truly considered to be Canadians.

It was in this climate that Normie

Kwong broke down barriers for Chinese Canadians in professional sports in Canada. He achieved a stature that his father and most other Chinese Canadians could only have dreamed of reaching.

2 The Unlikely Neighbourhood Star

The Kwong family was one of two Chinese families in Calgary's Riverside-Bridgeland area. Unlike many Chinese, they lived outside the familiar surroundings of the city's Chinatown. It was a struggle being different in a white community. It led to racism and discrimination against their family, including their children.

Normie's older sisters faced many more problems compared to their younger brother. They were not allowed to have certain jobs just because they were Chinese. They had a hard time in the white-dominated society.

Luckily for Normie, he wasn't troubled by the same level of racism. He was just one of the kids growing up in the neighbourhood.

"I was always somebody that was a little different," said Norm, comparing himself to other Chinese people. "Everybody accepted me as I spoke well."

Just like the rest of the kids in his neighbourhood, Normie liked to play sports. In those days they whooped it up on the local streets and vacant lots.

"That's where it all started," said Normie. "We would play all kinds of sports, but football was the most popular."

Normie liked that football was a physical sport. He could run fast, tackle other players, and be tackled himself. His mother didn't like football because she heard how tough it was. She feared for her small but stocky son's life.

Football is a physical sport, especially for the ball carrier. Normie's mom was scared for him because he was so much smaller than the other players.

"She was of the opinion I shouldn't play because there was contact involved and the other players were bigger than me," said Normie. "She didn't know that if you are agile, you could get around them."

Normie's mother didn't realize he was playing on his school football team until his name was printed in the newspaper after a game. He was so successful in his high-school football league and city junior football league, and he seemed to be enjoying playing so much, she finally went along with it.

Normie was just fifteen years old when he broke into the Calgary junior football league. He played for the North Hill Blizzards. Two years later Normie was one of the league's stars. He was the main factor behind his team's success.

Two thousand people came out regularly to the junior games — almost as many fans as at the pro Stampeders games. A lot of the people in the crowd had an eye on Norm. Not because he was the only Chinese player, but because he was the best player on the field.

"Kwong carried the major load in the North Hill victory," wrote the *Calgary Herald* newspaper after one game. "The hard plunging Chinese halfback ran for good gains all night and climaxed an all around good performance with two classy touchdown dashes. When Kwong wasn't picking his way into the clear for long gains he was driving through the line with Arrow players vainly trying to drag him down."

Normie's mother wanted a university education for her son. But, although university had been the goal, Norm got sidetracked.

"After I achieved some success, she realized there was no way she could stop me," said Normie about playing football.

Normie was voted the league's 1947 Most Valuable Player. It made him the hottest football prospect in the city. The Stampeders squad thought Normie might have a place on their roster.

Normie wondered what type of future he could have. His sisters faced many restrictions in their lives. Norm wondered if he would also face those same problems. That led him to think about a career in sport. He thought it would be difficult to be a professional or business person. Many would have thought it impossible for a Chinese Canadian to be a football star.

3 The Benchwarmer

Les Lear knew what success was all about. He played in four Grey Cup finals with the Winnipeg Blue Bombers. He also played with the National Football League's Cleveland Rams. He was the first Canadian to play in the NFL.

Lear became the Stampeders coach in 1948. He brought a new trend to Canadian football. He signed Americans to play for his team. Most teams didn't want American players, because they were paid more than Canadian players.

Lear only had so much to spend to put together a team. After signing a handful of Americans, he didn't have much money left to fill out the roster. So he scouted the western junior football teams for young athletes. These inexperienced players were talented and cheap.

Normie was one of the players Lear scouted for the team. At the training camp Normie was surrounded by older players. But he wasn't nervous. He knew his skills would earn him a spot on Calgary's lineup. He was right. He was picked for the team.

Normie was eighteen years old at the start of the 1948 season. His first-year salary was $250. He was the first Canadian of Chinese descent to play Canadian football professionally. That fact didn't come to his mind, so at the time he didn't consider himself special. He just wanted to play football.

Calgary Stampeders Origins

The first football team in Calgary was formed in 1891. The Stampeders club was formed in 1908. At first, they were named the Calgary Tigers. The club would also go by the Canucks, the 50th Battalion, Altomahs, and the Bronks. They took the Stampeders name on September 29, 1945. The name comes from the annual Calgary Stampede rodeo.

"I've been the first Asian in a lot of things. Being a pioneer isn't always easy and it can be intimidating to be the first one to break through a cultural barrier," said Normie years later. "I guess I am a role model to some people. I've never made a point of trying to be one. I've just been myself through my life."

At the start of the season, Lear scared Normie. The coach was a fanatic for conditioning. He terrorized the young player into the finest condition of his life.

Lear put the team through two-and-a-half-hour workouts daily.

"He was a coach like nobody's seen before," said Norm.

Lear honed and polished the Stampeders until they were invincible.

"This is a tough game and condition means everything in football," said Coach Lear. "The Stampeders are fit every time they take to the gridiron."

With a new lineup, the Stampeders found they had a renewed interest in the team. The crowds at pre-season games steadily grew larger. The team gave them a good reason to show up in force. Like on August 30, 1948, when the Stamps defeated the Blue Bombers 30–0.

"After Monday's game it appears obvious more stands will be needed at Mewata Stadium to accommodate the rapidly growing crowd," wrote the *Calgary Herald*. "Lear has put football on the map in Calgary in a big way and there is more interest in the pigskin sport than before."

The *Herald* even gave the Stamps a new nickname. They called them Les Lear and his Lambasters.

At the start of the season, Lear mainly used his veterans. His junior players were getting into shape and learning the professional game. As the season progressed, he slowly worked them into the lineup.

Normie didn't get much playing time in the Stampeders' lineup. He wasn't very happy about it. The season before, he was a junior-league star. The play always involved him. Normie could win a game by himself.

Since he wasn't playing much with the Stamps, he wanted to go back to juniors. He was still young enough to play junior football. He wanted to play football, not sit on the bench.

Lear had a hard time convincing him to

stay. Normie eventually agreed to finish the season and by mid-season he was playing more regularly for the Stamps.

Success on the field did not always guarantee respect for Normie. In his first pro season he faced racism on the field. He was often called "Chink" by his opponents. It was a common, hateful name used to put down Chinese people.

On the street, Chinese people were regularly called hurtful names. They were not playing in a game like Normie. They faced this hate simply because they were different. But Norm did not think his opponents were trying to discriminate against him.

"I don't think they were trying to hurt me," said Normie. "I just think they were trying to throw me off my game."

Young Normie and the Stampeders had a perfect regular season in 1948. They were unbeaten in twelve games.

They would face the Saskatchewan Roughriders in the western final. It was a two-game playoff. The team that scored the most points during the games would win the series. As western champs they would then challenge the eastern champions for the Grey Cup.

The first game of the western final was played in Regina. More than 100 Calgarians travelled to Regina to cheer on their team. That game unexpectedly ended in a 4–4 tie. The winner of the second game would go on to the Grey Cup in Toronto.

At the start of the season only a few thousand people were at Stampeders games. As the season progressed more and more people got excited about the team. The stands started to fill with numbers not seen before. At the final game of the 1948 western final, 10,000 people crammed into Calgary's Mewata Stadium. They had caught football fever.

The Stampeders didn't disappoint their hometown fans. They won the game 17–6. They were the first Calgary team since 1911 to win a western football final. It would be Calgary's first Grey Cup championship game.

4 Calgary's Big Game

The Stampeders boarded the eastbound train with the hopes of winning the Grey Cup. But the Stamps didn't impress the easterners. They didn't think this western challenger could defeat the eastern champion Ottawa Rough Riders. They said they were simply too small in size to compete.

Ottawa was the five-to-one favourite to win. The Stamps didn't let that bother them. Opinions didn't win games. They knew the only thing that mattered was the score on the scoreboard at the end of the game.

It took three days to travel to Toronto from Calgary. Coach Lear didn't want the ride to soften the team. They could get out of shape sitting all that time. So at every stop he made the players run laps around the train.

It was all one long adventure for Normie. He wasn't just going to play in the biggest game of his young career. It was his first time on a train. He had never been this far away from home. He would be sleeping in a hotel for the first time.

But Normie wouldn't get any chance to explore Toronto. Lear had a strict schedule for his team. From Toronto's Union Station he took them to nearby Oakville to train. They practised hard twice a day for six days. Lear whipped his collection of old pros and tough, junior-aged kids into top shape.

The Grey Cup

The Grey Cup trophy is awarded each year to the Canadian football champion. It was first played for in 1909 between two eastern Canadian teams. It wasn't until 1921 that the first western Canadian team played an eastern team for the national championship.

When Stampeders fans arrived at the game, they were dwarfed by the Grey Cup crowd of 20,000 at Toronto's Varsity Stadium.

There was a lot of attention on the game across Canada. Time stood still that afternoon back in Alberta. People sat around their radios to listen to the play-by-play.

All the attention could have made the Stampeders nervous. Most of them had never played in a game that was so important. They had never played in front of so many people. Worst of all, most of the people in the stands were cheering for Ottawa.

Coach Lear was especially worried about his younger players. But he had a plan.

"If my kids get nervous before the big crowd, I'm gonna go in and play and maybe stick around for a couple of plays. Just to settle them down," said Lear.

When his younger players got the jitters early, he went into the game like he promised. For 50 minutes he hit every Rough Riders player who came his way.

At nineteen, Normie was the youngest player ever to compete in the Grey Cup championship. For most of the game Norm watched from the bench. He was not part of Coach Lear's Grey Cup plans. But he was not totally forgotten. Lear still believed everybody should be part of the Grey Cup experience. He knew this game could be a historic event. He sent Normie out on to the field for three plays. Normie never touched the ball.

Sitting on the bench gave Normie a new goal. He vowed that if he ever returned to the Grey Cup it would be as a starter. At least Normie had a front-row seat to watch a landmark match. On that day Lear's Lambasters imprinted Calgary on the football map.

On the final whistle that day, the Stampeders had a 12–7 lead. Calgary won the Grey Cup. The fans surged on to the field. They took the Grey Cup and paraded it around the streets of Toronto. The celebration headed back to the Royal York lobby. It was a celebration that didn't end until the team and their supporters arrived back in Calgary.

This was more than just a Grey Cup victory. It was the start of a new feeling in the West.

"You could actually feel the adventurous western spirit beginning to build, to take shape. The spirit that lives on to this day," said Calgary player Norm Hill years later. "It was the beginning of Calgary in a sense. I don't just mean winning the Grey Cup. That game, what we accomplished was only a reflection of everything that was going on. There was a sense of progress in the city that whole year. The belief that anything was possible."

In the end, it all came down to Coach Les Lear. He put together this unbeatable team. He didn't realize that he played a role in the shaping of western Canadian sporting history that sunny afternoon. He only said that, "my kids came through for me."

By winning the Grey Cup, Normie earned a $250 bonus. Added to his 1948 regular season salary he made $500. His high school friends were unsure about their futures. Not Normie. He went from the school field to a Grey Cup final. He was officially a professional player.

5 First-String Starter

During the 1949 training camp, Normie focused on earning a starting position. First, he had to impress Coach Lear and show he was ready. Lear knew Normie had the potential to be a good player. The coach just needed to see him as an equal to the veterans.

People described Normie as a chunky, straight-ahead runner. He ran straight through the opposition's line of defense. From a distance it looked like there was no way through them. Normie would put his head down and find a way. He would disappear for a moment in a mass of bodies. Then he would pop out like a cork from those players and make constant gains down the field.

He became known as the player who could gain yards when given the ball. Lear saw Norm as the go-to-guy to run the ball in his offense. By the end of training camp Normie was named as a starting player. Normie also proved himself to other players and fans. He became a respected player whose race did not define him. It was a situation other Chinese Canadians dreamed about at the time.

With the growing popularity of the Stampeders, people reorganized football in nearby Edmonton. The 1949 season saw the return of the capital city to big-time football after a ten-year absence. They took on the name of the city's previous football club, the Edmonton Eskimos.

Rivalry occurred in every sport between Calgary and Edmonton, including football. Their first meeting opened the season on September 6, 1949. The Stampeders played like Grey Cup champions and won the game 20–6. It was a special game for Normie. He scored the first touchdown of his professional career. It happened when Calgary was making a drive down the field. The first play had Norm taking the ball through the centre of the opponent's line. With the opposition trying to tackle him he got rid of the ball. He lateral passed it to teammate Rod Pantages, who moved the play into Edmonton territory. Calgary's quarterback Keith Spaith then threw a long pass to Woody Strode to put the Stampeders into scoring position. On the next play, Normie was given the ball. With his head down, he could not get through to score a touchdown. But on the following play, Normie found a hole and plunged through to score.

Two weeks later, Calgary won 20–1 against the Blue Bombers. The most spectacular play of the game involved Normie. In the third quarter he caught the ball off a Winnipeg kick. He carried it up to his own 25-yard line. Pantages only gained four yards on the next play. Then the ball was given to Normie again. He started out on his own 29-yard line. He ran with the ball over the centre. He weaved his way through a maze of Bombers players. He outran Winnipeg's fastest players with his great speed. They only saw Normie's heels as he sped down the field. He rushed 75 yards for the touchdown.

While playing junior football Normie's nickname had been the "China Clipper." He was named after the fastest ship on any ocean. As a starter in Calgary, the China Clipper set sail again.

The Stampeders were once again the western Canadian champions. The defending Grey Cup champs had a chance to repeat their success.

The excitement in the West could not be contained. Two thousand Calgarians jammed the CPR station in Calgary to say goodbye to the Stampeders special train bound for Toronto. They weren't there to cheer for the team, but for the 300 shouting, happy fans who filled the train. They were travelling thousands of kilometres to watch a football game. To their amazement, people greeted the trainload of fans at every station stop across western Canada.

The 1949 Grey Cup was played before a sellout crowd of 21,000 at Toronto's Varsity Stadium. Calgary's opponents were the Montreal Alouettes. The Als were in their first Grey Cup game since 1931. They were led by quarterback Frankie

Filchock. He had played against Coach Lear when they were both in the NFL.

Montreal opened the scoring in the first quarter on a 75-yard touchdown drive down the field. On the following kickoff Montreal recovered the ball when Calgary's Norm Hill was hammered by the Als' Glen Douglas. Four plays later, Filchock threw a deep touchdown pass to make the score Montreal 11, Calgary 0.

Montreal soon added to their lead. With the ball on his own 39-yard line, Calgary's Keith Spaith called for a long pass. Sugarfoot Anderson sped down the field waiting for the pass. But before Spaith could get the throw off, Montreal's Herb Trawick slammed into him. The ball popped loose. Trawick grabbed it, shook off a Calgary player, and marched down into the Calgary end zone.

Normie played a much more important role for the Stamps in this Grey Cup. He didn't have any flashy touchdown plays. He just repeatedly plunged with the ball through the Montreal defensive line. He would gain three, five, and seven yards with each carry. This was important to get the team into scoring position.

In the third quarter, a penalty against Calgary set up another Montreal touchdown. Filchock threw a long pass to receiver Virgil Wagner. Calgary's Rod Pantages climbed into the air for an interception. Calgary celebrated until the judge of play penalized Pantages for interference. The Calgary coaching staff were angry. Montreal regained possession of the ball. Four plays later, Wagner smashed into the Calgary end zone. The score stood at Montreal 23, Calgary 7.

Both teams continued to play hard, but Montreal had the edge. When the final whistle went, they had won the Grey Cup, 28–15.

New Set of Eyes

Normie had a great 1949 season as a starter. It might have been because of a new product. He was nearsighted, so he could see things that were close, but not things that were far away. This made it difficult to see the ball. Off the field he wore thick, black-rimmed glasses. But he could not wear them playing. In 1949, contact lenses became available. He started to wear them during games. They didn't bother him and actually helped his play.

People across Canada came out to meet the Stamps as they returned to Calgary on the train. The crowds were out to show the team they were there for them in defeat as well as in victory.

"I never figured people along the way would greet us the way they did," said Coach Lear.

Thirty thousand people greeted the Stamps back in Calgary. They lined the train station tracks waiting for a glimpse of the players.

"When you greet us like this, when we're beaten, I hate to think what would have happened had we come back home with the Cup," said Normie.

For Normie, the most important person in that crowd was his mother. She waited at the depot for the train to return. When it arrived she wasted no time in getting aboard and finding her son. She wanted to welcome him home and say how proud she was of him.

6 Injury Scare

It seemed like life couldn't get any better for Normie. The newspapers said he was one Stampeder who should have an outstanding year in 1950. They loved to write about how he smashed through the opponent's defensive line.

"Norm Kwong . . . There were a couple of times when he literally flashed through the defensive line," wrote the *Calgary Herald*. "The timing, blocking and Kwong's running were so perfectly integrated that he was through their secondary before they knew what happened."

Normie was even offered a chance to join the San Francisco 49ers of the NFL. He turned them down. There would have been no financial gain in going to the United States because he was a young player.

The Alouettes travelled west for a series of pre-season exhibition games. One game was a replay of the 1949 Grey Cup final.

Calgary was out to reverse their Grey Cup defeat. The final outcome was decided by Normie's plunging drive. He put his head down and ran through the Montreal defensive line for a touchdown. The Stamps' hometown crowd was excited when they won 19–7.

But a turn of events during the game changed the season for both the Stampeders and Normie. Normie injured his ankle during the game. At first it didn't look serious. He carried the ball for two first downs and a touchdown.

"Very little information is available as to just how bad Kwong's ankle really is," wrote the *Herald*, "but all are hoping, including Kwong, that the injury isn't serious."

After that game Normie didn't take part in any practices. The season was only a week away. Nobody knew if Normie would start. The Stamps were quiet about the situation. They were a team made up of old veterans. They were looking toward the youngsters as the future. At twenty, Normie was a part of that future. Unfortunately, it didn't look very good.

"The lad that will be missed most is Normie Kwong. He should have had, and is hoped to still have, an outstanding season," wrote the *Herald* right before the start of the season. "This is based on both his performance last season and in practices to date."

Normie was not in the lineup to start

the Stamps' season. Their opening game was against provincial rivals, the Eskimos. Edmonton trampled Calgary 18–8.

The Stampeders began the season as the worst team in the league. The 1949 Grey Cup finalists started the 1950 season with eight losses in nine starts. They looked for something to change things around. They needed Normie back in the lineup.

It was a hard time for Normie. His career was suddenly in serious trouble. Athletes don't always come back from injuries. Norm had the determination to come back — he just needed his body to heal. If it didn't, his football career would end before it really began.

It took a month for Normie to recover. He played his first game against the Blue Bombers on October 1, 1950. Normie didn't instantly transform the Stampeders back into winners. They lost 22–0.

In the next game, Normie did play a role

in a Stampeders victory. His play helped them defeat the Roughriders 16–13.

"Special praise must be given to Normie Kwong," wrote the *Herald*. "The likeable lad came back to haunt the Riders as he ran and fought with his old speed and tenacity. The China Clipper's injury was a terrific blow to Calgary's hopes, for just his being on the field raised Stampeder stock by at least twenty per cent."

Normie's return could not turn around the Stamps' fortunes. They did not make the western playoff. Some reporters said the Stamps had the most disappointing season in the history of Canadian football.

Calgary was looking to make some changes. They didn't want that season to repeat itself in 1951. They signed new players and traded away others. The most surprising trade involved Normie being sent to his rivals, the Eskimos.

During the off-season, Calgary team

officials had been told that Normie's ankle injury was career-ending. He would be worthless if he was injured. So they traded him for a healthy player. Edmonton's gain would be Calgary's loss.

They were once opponents, but Normie was quickly accepted by Edmonton fans. At first, the trade hurt his feelings. He was from Calgary and his hometown team gave up on him. For the first time in his life he had to move away from home. But he soon felt he was in a place where he was wanted.

7 Battle of Alberta

The Calgary versus Edmonton rivalry has been going on almost since the two cities were first settled. This friendly rivalry was, and still is, played out through sports. People refer to it as the "Battle of Alberta."

In the summer the two cities competed in baseball. In the winter they battled it out playing hockey. In the fall the football field was their battleground.

The Battle of Alberta was going strong in the 1951 football season. The critics thought Calgary had the edge over the Eskimos. They were dismissed by the other western clubs as not being a threat. But during their 1951 training camp Edmonton put together a team that would change all opinions of them.

Eskimos coach Annis Stukas started by signing Alouettes champion Frankie Filchock. With all his experience he became the leader on the field.

Alongside him were two new speedsters. Normie and Rollie Miles joined Mike King to make up the most devastating ground attack in Canada.

Normie's skills were known when he started pre-season training. Miles was a complete unknown to everybody, even the coaching staff. He asked if he could try out. They almost said no. It would have been a mistake because he proved to be a great player. Miles made the starting lineup as a halfback.

The Eskimos started the season on top of the league standings. They won three and lost only once. Normie's hard running with the ball was a factor in that success.

In their first game against the Stampeders, Normie's 45-yard touchdown drive was an example of sheer grit. He was hit by five different Stampeders, but he just refused to stop. In a game against the Roughriders one week later, he carried the ball fourteen times and scored two touchdowns.

Normie had been traded for Reg Clarkson. Reg was a good player, but not as good as Normie. Normie wanted to show that fact every time he played against Calgary. He made sure he played at the top of his game.

"Every time he carried the ball Stampeder fans just held their heads and bemoaned a bad bargain for Calgary," wrote the *Edmonton Journal* after one game. "He is one of the most dazzling runners in the game."

The final game of the regular season pitted the Eskimos against the Stampeders. It had been a full season since Normie was traded. He wanted this game to be a reminder of what Calgary lost.

"Here was a gritty gridder who was the carrier of many a Calgary chuckle at Edmonton's expense back in the summer. The Stamps thought they were putting one over the Eskimos when they let Kwong go in a straight trade for Reg Clarkson," wrote the *Journal*. "But, Clarkson missed most of the season through injuries of his own and Kwong once more has been one of the most brilliant gallopers in the league."

Edmonton's running game was a nightmare for the Stampeders. Normie and his teammates carried the ball on almost every play. The player with the ball looked for openings to run through. The other players blocked opponents to make that opening possible. It was a very physical way to play the game.

On one play Normie did it all himself. He received the ball on Edmonton's 43-yard line. He rushed down the field, running through the holes that were created for him. He shook off a couple of defenders wanting to tackle him. Only one player was left and Normie dodged around him. It was a dramatic 67-yard touchdown run.

By the end of the 1951 season, Normie set a new league rushing record. He rushed for 933 yards. He also scored eight touchdowns and finished tenth in league scoring. For his efforts, he was selected as a Western First Team All-Star.

The western final pitted the Eskimos against the Roughriders. It was a best-of-three-games playoff. Edmonton won the first game 15–11. They were one game away from the Grey Cup final. Almost

600 Edmonton fans travelled to Regina to watch the second game. The Eskimos gave it everything they had, but the Roughriders were too strong. The Riders won 12–5.

Game three was a close one. The Roughriders were leading 8–0 with 15 minutes left to go in the fourth quarter. Both teams started to make offensive charges down the field. Edmonton scored three touchdowns. It was not enough as the Roughriders added two touchdowns to their score.

By the final whistle, the Roughriders held a slight edge and won 19–18. Saskatchewan won the series 2–1 and were named western champions. They were headed for the Grey Cup.

The Eskimos were only three seasons old. They were only one game away from the Grey Cup. Their fans were not sad about the loss. They celebrated the team

The Edmonton Eskimos were just getting started in 1951. Normie would play an important part in that success.

when they returned from Regina.

At the crowded Edmonton celebration, Normie said, "Gosh, maybe we did win after all."

8 Edmonton's Time to Shine

Despite his outstanding play, Normie figured he was lucky to play professional football. By 1952 the league had changed. It was home to more veteran American players. They were former top college and professional NFL players. Canadian football leagues offered them another place to play. Unfortunately, with more Americans coming north, there were fewer roster spots available for Canadians.

"It's tougher now than in 1948 for

a junior to break in," said Norm. "It's getting tougher every year."

He knew he had to be at the top of his game. There were many American players looking to take his job.

Quarterback Frankie Filchock was named the new Eskimos coach in 1952. He shared his quarterback duties with American Claude Arnold.

The 1952 season wasn't shaping into anything special. By September 2, the Eskimos had only one win. They had beat the Stampeders 17–10. Otherwise, they lost two games and had one tie. It was the start critics thought they would have.

Any team in a slump looks to their next game to turn things around. The Eskimos looked to turn their season around during their game on September 8 against the Blue Bombers.

The Bombers opened the scoring in the first quarter with a touchdown. In the second quarter Normie finished off an Eskimos drive down the field to score Edmonton's first touchdown. Before the end of the first half the Bombers scored another touchdown. They took the lead 12–6.

After the third quarter, Winnipeg still held the lead. The Eskimos' Joe Aquirre had scored a touchdown, but the Bombers had answered back by kicking a field goal. Bombers 15, Eskimos 12.

At the beginning of the fourth quarter, the Eskimos started a drive down the field. An offensive drive had many different parts. They included different players on the team. This drive started as Eskimos player Jumbo Chambers rushed the ball down the field. His longest rush was a 38-yard drive that put the Eskimos on the Bombers 17-yard line. Rollie Miles then grabbed a pass from Arnold on the next play. He took the ball ten yards to

CANADIAN
FOOTBALL
ILLUSTRATED 1956
35c

NORMIE KWONG
Schenley Award Winner
"Canadian Player of the Year"

ALL
STARS

ACTION
PHOTOS

RECORDS

SCHEDULES

Normie became a fan favourite with his increased success on the field.

the Bombers' seven-yard line. On the next play, Normie was given the ball and sped towards the end zone. Rollie Prather made a key block to open a path for Normie to run through the Bombers players. His touchdown put the Eskimos ahead for the first time in the game. They held out that lead and thought they might just get the victory.

The Bombers' quarterback knew he wasn't beaten until the final bell rang. He still had time for one more drive down the field. In the dying moments of the game the Bombers scored another touchdown. It was the game-winner. Winnipeg won 21–18. That loss put the Eskimos dead last in the league standings.

Coach Filchock saw that his team needed a boost on the field. So he entered the next game against the Roughriders. He helped lead his team to their second win of the season.

"Coach Frank Filchock's dramatic appearance last night appeared to supply the spark that the Eskimos needed to escape permanent relegation to the cellar," wrote the *Journal*.

Filchock's heroics continued into the next game against Winnipeg. The Bombers were looking to extend a four-game winning streak. They took a 9–0 lead into the last quarter.

Rollie Prather scored one touchdown for the Eskimos. He received the ball after hitting it out of the hands of a Bombers ball carrier. The winning touchdown came when Normie caught a pass from Filchock. He ran into the end zone without trouble.

Normie always wanted to put on a show when he played his old team. On September 22, Norm scored three touchdowns against his former teammates. The Eskimos won 35–18 — their third straight victory. By the end of September they climbed to second place.

The Eskimos turned their early troubles around and made it into the western playoffs. In the semi-finals they defeated the Stampeders. They advanced to face the Bombers in the western final.

Edmonton's Clarke Stadium held 15,424 fans who came out to watch the first game of the western final. Edmonton had lost the previous two western final series. Everybody wanted this to be their year to win.

"Maybe this fall. It's going to be different. It's gotta be," said Frank Morris, Edmonton's defensive guard.

The large hometown crowd did not help the Eskimos. The Bombers won 28–12. The final two games of the series would be played in Winnipeg.

Winnipeg and their heroes, the Bombers, were confident they would play for the

Grey Cup. They thought the second game with the Eskimos was just a formality. They were sure of their own victory.

But the Eskimos won 18–12. The series was tied. The headline in the paper the next day read: "Winnipeg Fans, Players Show Signs of Panic."

"The only person who thought Edmonton had a chance of winning were the Eskimos themselves," wrote the *Journal*.

In the final game the Eskimos outplayed, outwitted, and out-thought the Bombers. Edmonton won 22–11. For their great effort, they were awarded the western championship. For the first time since 1922, a team from Edmonton would play in the Grey Cup. They would face the Toronto Argonauts for the national championship.

The excitement of Calgary's 1948 Grey Cup trip was duplicated by Eskimos fans. A train named the Grey Cup Special hauled twelve carloads full of fans to Toronto.

One thousand people were waiting at Toronto's Union Station to greet them.

The Eskimos opened the scoring late in the first quarter. Normie ran hard with the ball. He ran around the Argos' offensive line and scored the game's first touchdown.

The Argos answered quickly in the second quarter. Toronto's Nobby Wirkowski had his own scoring rush for a touchdown. They then kicked the convert to give them a 6–5 lead. Soon afterwards they scored another touchdown and kicked a field goal.

Late in the third quarter, the Eskimos trimmed Toronto's lead. Edmonton's quarterback controlled the play as his team marched down the field. Play after play, the Eskimos gained yards to put them closer to the Toronto end zone. From the Argos ten-yard line Normie took the ball. Teammates Rollie Prather and Mario De Marco blocked the opposition from getting at Norm. He scored his second touchdown of the game.

In the last quarter, the Eskimos' assault continued. Arnold guided his team to the Argo 17-yard line. He got them within distance for another touchdown. On the next play, he was trapped behind the line of scrimmage. Arnold tried not to get hit, but an Argos player tackled him. The ball came loose and a Toronto player recovered it.

By the end of the fourth quarter, Toronto scored another touchdown. Toronto won the Grey Cup game 21–11.

The Eskimos were looking toward the next season. They still thought they had a team that could win the big game.

9 A Football Revolution

The Eskimos wanted to win the Grey Cup. They thought they had the team to do it. But they needed the right coach. So they replaced Filchock with Darrell Royal.

Royal came to the Eskimos from the University of Oklahoma. He was an assistant coach under head coach Bud Wilkinson. Bud was a football innovator. He changed how football was played. This change involved how the offensive line positioned themselves at the line of scrimmage. It was known as the split-t formation. Royal was about to introduce it to Canadian football.

At the time, most teams employed a "t" formation. The offensive linemen crouched shoulder-to-shoulder, thrusting forward to power defenders aside. This created holes for the running backs to run through. Brute strength was needed to move the defenders out of the way.

In the split-t formation, the offensive linemen spaced themselves a little over one metre part. The defenders had to equal this separation distance. The offensive linemen had an easier time blocking the defenders. This created bigger holes for the ball carriers to run through.

With the split-t, a team's running game could be unstoppable. They could gain longer yardage down the field with each carry. This made the offensive attack much more of a threat.

When Royal came to Edmonton they thought he was crazy. They didn't think football should be played that way. They didn't think it would work. It took Royal two league starts, and two straight victories, to convince people he was right.

"If Darrell Royal accomplished nothing more in Canada, he will go down in the books as a young man who revolutionized Canadian football," wrote the *Journal*.

This new split-t system played well to Normie's strength. He loved barrelling through the middle of all the players for long yardage gains. He usually had to smash his body against opponents to get by them. Now, he had a little more room to run. One game he rushed for 92 yards, and, in another game, he went for 133 yards. He picked up many important first downs and scored touchdowns with his running power.

Coach Royal's split-t formation made the Eskimos into a strong and exciting

With the split-t formation Normie would have many record-setting seasons.

team to watch. The Eskimos finished the regular season in first place with a 12–4 record. Unfortunately, they lost out in the western final against the Blue Bombers.

The fans in Edmonton thought Coach Royal would lead the Eskimos to a 1954 Grey Cup victory. But he got a better offer to coach at the University of Mississippi. Royal was gone, along with the hopes of all Eskimos fans.

Frank Ivy was signed to coach the Eskimos in 1954. He had never coached Canadian football, but neither had Royal. Both coaches came from the same school of football.

Ivy was a former NFL player. He was tall and went bald young, so his nickname was Pop. Like Royal, he was a coach at the University of Oklahoma with Bud Wilkinson. He was also a split-t expert. The Eskimos would not be losing their winning formation.

Pop Ivy's greatest skill was his eye for talent. He wanted to add to the Eskimos' roster. He already had offensive superstars in Normie and Miles. He thought he needed a few more. The signing of two important players changed western football. Jackie Parker and Johnny Bright would help transform the Eskimos into one of Canadian football's greatest teams.

10 A Battle to the End

The signing of Jackie Parker received the least amount of attention. He was Pop Ivy's secret. Parker was a quarterback from Mississippi State University. But he was signed to the Eskimos as a running back.

American Bernie Faloney was supposed to be the starting quarterback. But that plan was thrown out the window when he injured his ankle in an exhibition game. Quarterback duties were solely on backup Claude Arnold. He lost his first game against the Roughriders 21–13. Then he got injured in his next game against the Blue Bombers. Halfback Rollie Miles filled in for Arnold in a 7–3 defeat.

The Eskimos lost their first two games of the regular season. They also lost both of their quarterbacks. They would not play another game for two weeks. During that time Ivy devised a new plan. It centred around his secret from Mississippi State.

Jackie Parker was named the first-string quarterback.

The *Edmonton Journal* asked Pop why he hadn't given Parker a shot at the quarterback position earlier in the season. Didn't he think Parker was a good quarterback?

"Certainly," Ivy said, "I knew he was a good quarterback. He was the best quarterback in the tough Southeast Conference in college. But he can also run with the ball from the halfback slot.

He was my insurance. The insurance will now begin to pay off."

The Eskimos faced the B.C. Lions after their two week break. It was Edmonton's first victory of the season, 12–6.

A couple of days later they faced the Stampeders. It was in this game that Parker impressed everybody with his play. The Eskimos won 30–11. Parker did nearly everything and did it well.

"Quarterback Jackie Parker made a shamble of the Stampeders and took a stranglehold on the imagination of the Eskimo fans," wrote the *Journal*.

By the end of September, halfway through the season, the Eskimos had their full roster back. Faloney at quarterback, Miles and Parker at halfback, and Normie at fullback.

During a 12–8 victory over the Bombers, fans got to see a new play. The Edmonton offense perfected the fake

The 1954 Edmonton Eskimos were the first of many championship teams. Norm wore number 95.

hand-off. At the centre of it was the China Clipper. Faloney would fake the hand-off to Normie and then slip the ball to Parker. Parker ran a first down while the opposition tackled the China Clipper.

As the season went on, Normie came to be known as the faker. He would also regularly run for 80, 90, or 100 yards in a game. He picked up first downs with his running power. But it was for his faking that he was remembered.

"The China Clipper is one of the few pigskin practitioners around and about who is sometimes more successful at not carrying the ball than he is when laden with leather," wrote the *Journal*.

Normie's importance to the Eskimos was shown when his fellow players voted him co-captain of the team. It was a post he kept until he retired.

The Eskimos rose through the standings as the season progressed. By mid-October they were in second place. After the final game, a 21–12 victory over the Bombers, the Eskimos were on top of the western football standings.

It seemed like every year the Eskimos faced the Bombers in the western final. It was the same matchup in 1954. This series could go to either team.

Edmonton and Winnipeg had a history of hard fought western final matches. The Eskimos won the first game 9–3. The

Bombers won the second game 12–6.

The winner of a trip to the Grey Cup came down to one game. That game was played in Edmonton in front of a capacity crowd. The Eskimos had poured everything they had into the previous two games. Many of their players were injured.

"The Eskimos were seven parts desire and three parts tape, bandages, casts, splints and braces holding together their bruised, battered bodies," wrote the *Journal*. "The desire that wouldn't be denied was forged in the fire of defeat in Winnipeg."

But all the injured players were still in the lineup. Coach Ivy asked the healthy players to carry the offensive load. He decided to concentrate his running attack on Normie. He was called upon to carry the ball often. He came through like a champion. Normie rushed for more than half of the 252 yards the Eskimos gained in rushing.

The Bombers led 2–1 at the end of the first quarter. The Eskimos rebounded to take a 7–2 lead at halftime. A Bombers field goal made the game closer again at 7–5. By the final whistle, Edmonton added a field goal to win 10–5. They were going to the Grey Cup.

After the game, the players were even more tired and hurt. They sat in pain knowing they had accomplished something good.

Down one darkened locker corridor, Normie bowed his head and sobbed, "I never wanted to win one so much." He threw off the tension that had carried him through one of the greatest games he had ever played in Edmonton.

The Eskimos now had only one more game to play. The players had to push aside any pain they felt. They had to be a determined bunch if they wanted to win the Grey Cup.

11 The Western Underdogs

The Alouettes were the strongest team in eastern Canada. They swamped all opposition. They easily won their spot in the Grey Cup Championship Game. They played a wide-open brand of football. Their quarterback, Sam "The Rifle" Etchevarry, filled the air with well-placed passes. Receivers Hal Patterson and Red O'Quinn managed to catch many of them.

Normie and the Eskimos played a more physical brand of football. They liked to run with the ball. They ran around their opponents. They also tried to run right through them to gain yards or score a major. It was a gritty, tough style of football.

Easterners didn't think the Eskimos had a chance to win the Grey Cup. Toronto reporters, especially, were not kind to the westerners.

Bunny Morganson of the *Toronto Telegram* wrote, "Tell me, why are they bothering to bring Edmonton east for the game?"

No easterner predicted an Edmonton victory. They didn't seem to take the Eskimos seriously.

Western teams always had the disadvantage of travelling for a Grey Cup game. They had a long trip, a change of climate, and unfamiliar playing fields.

Normie and the Eskimos entered the Grey Cup game as underdogs. They were labelled a "two-dollar football team." They were given little chance of defeating the Alouettes.

Edmonton started the game with a touchdown. After marching the ball to the Montreal three-yard line, Rollie Miles accepted a pitchout from Bernie Faloney. Miles wanted to throw, but was unable to find a receiver. Soon a swarm of Alouettes defenders trapped him 25 yards behind the line of scrimmage. A sack of Miles seemed likely when suddenly teammate Bob Dean levelled Montreal's Herb Trawick. The block gave Miles additional time and he threw the ball to Earl Lindly for a touchdown.

A few minutes later Montreal scored on a record-setting touchdown pass. At the Montreal 20-yard line, Etchevarry gunned a short pass to O'Quinn. While the pass was high, O'Quinn reached up to make an over-the-head, one-handed catch. Edmonton defenders, amazed by the catch, stood frozen, admiring the grab. This allowed O'Quinn to race away for a 90-yard touchdown.

Faloney came back with his own drive. After moving the ball 85 yards down the field, Faloney ran a quarterback sneak. At the Montreal one-yard line, Faloney tried to run for the touchdown. His initial attempt was stopped. Then, after a shove by Normie, Faloney ran into the end zone.

Edmonton held a 14–6 lead early in the second quarter. That was until Montreal took control of the game. Etchevarry led another 100-yard drive, which ended with a touchdown by O'Quinn.

A few minutes later, Montreal's quarterback assembled a 90-yard touchdown drive. This time Chuck Hunsinger scored the major on a short pass. This gave Montreal an 18–14 lead.

Montreal scored the only point of the third quarter. They showed no signs of losing their lead in the fourth when Etchevarry threw for another touchdown.

The Alouettes soon had a chance to put

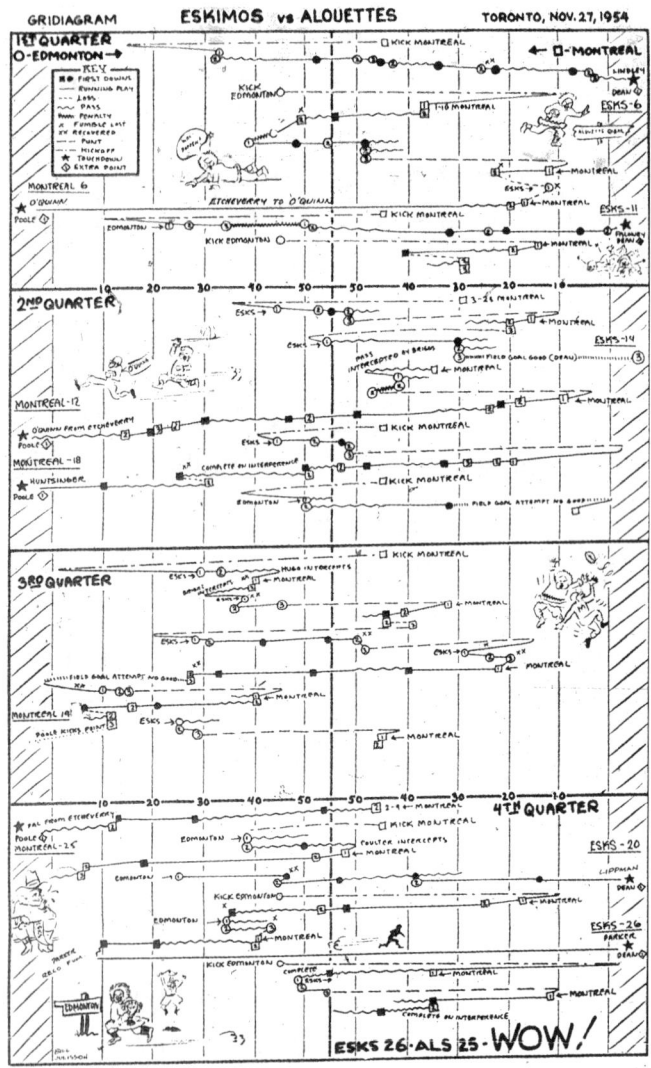

ESKIMOS vs ALOUETTES — TORONTO, NOV. 27, 1954

ESKS 26 · ALS 25 — WOW!

the game out of reach. Montreal drove the ball to the Edmonton seven-yard line. With a third down and four yards to go, a field goal would have increased Montreal's lead to 14 points. The coach decided to take a chance. He didn't kick the ball. The gamble failed and sparked the Eskimos.

They took possession of the ball on their own 25-yard line. Edmonton stormed downfield. A risky third-down play put the ball on the Montreal 27-yard line. Three plays later, Glenn Lippmann exploited a gaping hole in the Montreal line. He rushed 14 yards for a touchdown. The Als still led 25–20.

Montreal was in no danger of losing. There was little time remaining in the game. They would win if they didn't make

Opposite Page: This illustrates the play during the 1954 Grey Cup game. The lines show where the ball was carried down the field in each quarter.

any foolish mistakes.

It looked like the reporters were right. The Alouettes were on the verge of winning the Grey Cup.

With the time ticking down, Montreal advanced the ball to Edmonton's 10-yard line. It looked like they would score another touchdown.

Alouette Chuck Hunsinger was given the ball. He started up the field with teammates Herb Trawick and Ray Poole blocking. Quickly, Hunsinger was caught from behind.

An Eskimos defender grabbed Hunsinger by the legs. Rollie Prather hit him hard high up. When Prather hit him, the ball came out of his hands. It was considered a fumble. The ball bounced right in front of Jackie Parker.

Parker was the star of the 1954 regular season. But by the Grey Cup game he was badly injured. He had a chipped bone in his foot that stabbed him like a sword with every step. His knees were also battered and bruised. He could hardly walk. But he still wanted to play.

"My first intention was to fall on it," said Parker. "But there wasn't anybody else there, so I followed the ball and when it took a little hop I picked it up. I hesitated for just a split-second and somebody hollered, 'Go Jackie, Go'."

"I just took off out there, heading on a line for the corner of the field and the goalposts," Parker continued. "I felt I was home free when I had about 20 yards to go and I sneaked a quick look over my shoulders."

He saw that nobody was running after him. He thought they'd call the play back. His touchdown run wouldn't have counted. He ran the last ten yards slowly, afraid to look around again to see if they called it back.

"When I did look around, after crossing the line, the official had his arm up and I knew that no matter what happened in the next couple of minutes, we'd won the Grey Cup," Parker concluded.

Dean, who never missed a kick all season, split the goalposts with his kick for the extra point. Edmonton took the lead 26–25. A couple of minutes later the Edmonton Eskimos were Grey Cup champions. It was the first time in six years that a western team had won the Grey Cup.

When the game was over, Edmonton fans ran to the Eskimos' bench. Some of them lifted Normie onto their shoulders. He had a great game as he crashed through the Alouettes' line 13 times to gain 73 yards in rushing. He was carried off the field as they all celebrated the victory.

The Eskimos played like a team. They were fuelled by the negative opinions of eastern reporters.

"Maybe the fact sportswriters who called us a two-dollar team before we even got into town made us just peeved enough that we were going to win despite all our hurt," said one Eskimos player.

The Eskimos were not just playing against the Alouettes. They were also playing against the pain they felt. Four men played with broken bones and another with cracked ribs. Most others had bruises, sprains, cuts, and pure pain.

Eagle Keys was an example of that determination. He broke his leg during the first quarter of the game. That didn't stop him from playing. Time and time again he hopped back in on one leg to snap the ball for punts, field goal tries, and converts.

The Eskimos returned home champions. They were given a hero's welcome. One hundred and fifty thousand people turned out to cheer them on in a parade through the streets of Edmonton. School was let out early so kids could watch the parade. Work came to a standstill as the parade

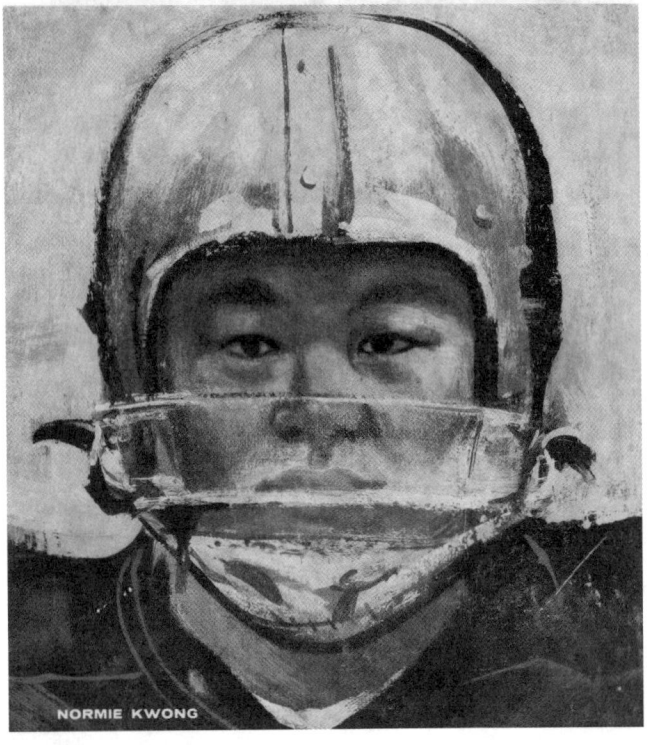

GREY CUP

CANADA'S SPORTS CLASSIC 50¢

NORMIE KWONG

Norm was an all-star player during the regular season.
He would become a legend by appearing in seven
Grey Cup championship games.

moved through the city.

It was an exciting time. It wasn't just that the Eskimos had won it for the West. It was the way they had won it. They were the underdogs and they came up with a tremendous fighting display that captured the public's imagination. People in the West wondered if it would be repeated in 1955.

From Radio to Small Screen

Hockey Night in Canada announcer Foster Hewitt broadcasted the first Grey Cup over the radio in 1930. The first televised Grey Cup game was in 1952. One Toronto station broadcast that game. Only televisions within range of the station could watch it. In 1953, three stations carried the game. By 1956 the CBC's live television network reached west to Winnipeg. People from Edmonton travelled to Winnipeg to watch the live Grey Cup game on television that year. In 1957 the game was televised coast to coast.

12 Kwong's Last Stand

Pop Ivy wanted another Grey Cup success. The fans expected it too. But it would be difficult. After the 1954 Grey Cup final, quarterback Bernie Faloney joined the Hamilton Tiger-Cats.

Like a puzzle, Pop had to put together a team, piece by piece. Each player was an important piece and together they were a single football force.

He moved Jackie Parker to the quarterback position. That left a hole at halfback. Pop paired Rollie Miles with Earl Lindley.

Pop knew he needed a new plan to create offense. Parker wouldn't be able to run the ball as much. Ivy needed somebody who could. He decided to change how the Eskimos played football. Every team played with one fullback. He was the player who gained yards by running up the middle, right through the opposition. Pop already had the best fullback in the game with Normie. But Ivy wanted to add to that offensive charge. So he created the new double-fullback formation. The Eskimos were the only football team using two fullbacks. They had the two best fullbacks in Canada in Normie and Johnny Bright.

In the first game under the double-fullback formation, the duo rushed for a combined 218 yards. They carried the Eskimos' ground attack to their opponents with a devastating show of power.

In the next game, the two players made the double-fullback system work to perfection. They were an unstoppable force against the B.C. Lions. The newspaper compared them to unstoppable human projectiles.

The Eskimos moved for a touchdown the first time they got their hands on the ball in the first quarter. Not a pass was thrown on their drive down the field. Bright and Normie, alternating like pistons in an engine, powered the ball down the field. Normie set-up the touchdown with a twisting 15-yard gallop to the B.C. five-yard line. Bright drove over into the end zone to score the major.

By the end of the first quarter, the Eskimos added another touchdown to lead 12–0.

The Eskimos shrugged off a B.C. touchdown in the second quarter. They turned around and promptly moved for their third touchdown. Miles started his drive with a 60-yard rush down the field. From the 54-yard line Parker, Bright, and Miles combined to take the play to the B.C. 26-yard line. On the third down, with three yards to go for the first down, the Eskimos should have kicked for a field goal. Instead, they gambled on the play. Parker passed to an Eskimos receiver, who ran to B.C.'s six-yard line. Normie then took a hand-off from Parker and chugged the ball over into the end zone.

At the end of the third quarter, Normie carried on five of seven plays as the Eskimos drove down the field for their fourth touchdown. He slammed through for gains of 19, 13, and 10 yards before polishing it off with a one-yard drive for the touchdown. The Eskimos led 24–6.

"Between them, the Esks fullbacks make Frank Ivy's new double-fullback system look like a work of art, racked up 278 of the 321 yards the Eskimos gained rushing briskly along the ground," wrote the *Journal*, after the Eskimos' 29–12 victory over the Lions. Normie ran for 148 yards and Bright ran for 130 yards.

The Edmonton backfield offered a potent offensive package. It had the sheer speed of Parker, Miles, and Lindly and the unbridled power of Bright and Normie. Normie was the only Canadian playing in the Eskimos starting offense.

Early in the 1955 season, a battle developed between Winnipeg's Gerry James and Normie. They were fighting for the all-time single season rushing record. For most of the season Normie was the rushing leader, but James was always close behind. Normie set the record in 1951 at 933 yards rushing. That mark was smashed in 1954 by Calgary's Howard Waugh. He rushed for 1,043 yards.

Normie had 436 yards just five games into the season. After eight games his rushing total stood at 650 yards.

"I figure I've got to average about 70 yards a game," said Normie, "and at that rate I cannot afford any injuries."

In the 1955 regular season, even when the Eskimos played poorly they would still win. By October 10, they had won twelve straight games. Not one team could match their offensive power. On October 12, they faced the B.C. Lions. Normie scored two touchdowns and rushed for 124 yards in a 38–2 victory. He needed only 71 yards for the new rushing record.

Normie set the rushing record against the Blue Bombers. His season total was at 1,055 yards — 12 yards more than the previous mark. James was still close behind. He had two more games to play, while Normie only had one. In James's extra game he overtook Norm's record.

Each player had one game left in the season. James would play his game first. He would set the mark Normie would have to smash in his final game.

Behind closed doors the team secretly wanted Normie to set the rushing record. They were prepared to do whatever it took to make it happen. But to the media they said they didn't plan on concentrating on individual records.

"It would be nice for Normie if it comes about," said Coach Ivy. "Kwong really works for every yard he makes. But as a team, it is difficult to be interested in individual records when the team work must be the goal."

The newspapers were calling the Eskimos' last game, "Kwong's Last Stand."

Normie openly admitted that he was shooting for a record. In James's last game, he rushed for 133 yards. Normie was faced with the task of overcoming a 149-yard handicap. Only a superhuman effort could beat such odds.

His teammates did everything they could to help Normie reach his goal. Behind the inspired blocking of his teammates, Normie was a crashing, relentless force that would not be denied. The whole team was fired up by the challenge of his uphill battle for the rushing record.

"It was a tribute to Kwong," said one reporter, "his teammates wanted the record for him and worked for it has hard as he did."

Normie slashed for 100 yards in the first half of the game. He rammed his way for another 92 in the balance of the game. James's record was toppled early in the fourth quarter.

"It was a wonderful thing," said Normie after the game. "I couldn't have done it without the team."

Normie set not one, but four new

rushing records. He established an all-time, one-season rushing record of 1,250 yards. Along the way he racked up an official one-game rushing record of 192 yards. He also had the most ball carries in a single game and set the record for the whole season.

Two weeks later, the Eskimos defeated the Bombers in the western final. For a second year the Eskimos would represent the West at the Grey Cup. They wouldn't have to travel far to play. Instead of the traditional eastern Grey Cup game, it would be played in Vancouver.

The eastern team was now at the disadvantage.

13 Not a Fluke

For the first time, the Grey Cup final would be played in western Canada. It had only been played in the East and mostly in Toronto. That had been a source of jealousy in the West. In 1955, Vancouver promised a much bigger crowd then the 27,000 maximum, which Toronto had provided.

The Eskimos had something to prove. Eastern reporters and football fans said the Eskimos were lucky to win the Grey Cup in 1954 — and that their victory was a fluke. The Eskimos wanted to show that they were no fluke team.

The crowd of 39,417 was the largest in Grey Cup history. Vancouver's newly built Empire Stadium was filled to capacity. For many fans it would be their first Grey Cup game.

Montreal took an early 1–0 lead in the game. Then the Eskimos scored the game's first touchdown on a 12-play, 85-yard drive. The feature play on the drive was by Normie. He prevented a Montreal touchdown by recovering a fumble by Parker on his own 25-yard line. Then the Eskimos passed and rushed their way down the field. Norm finished off the drive by scoring a touchdown.

Montreal quickly answered back. Using a mixture of strong running and good passing plays, Etchevarry drove the Alouettes to the Edmonton one-yard line. From there

Montreal's Pat Abbruzzi plunged into the end zone. Montreal took a 7–6 lead.

In the last minute of the first quarter, Montreal extended its lead. After Montreal's Jim Mills recovered a fumble on the Edmonton 42-yard line, Etchevarry threw a long pass to Hal Patterson. Patterson caught the pass behind an Eskimos defender and, in a couple of strides, he crossed the Edmonton goal line.

A turnover led to Edmonton's next score. With Montreal threatening to score another touchdown, Etchevarry lost ball possession on the Edmonton 29-yard line. Four plays later Johnny Bright took a hand-off from Jackie Parker. He couldn't be stopped by the Montreal tacklers and scored a touchdown.

Montreal replied by driving the ball to the Edmonton 15-yard line. Facing a second down and inches, Edmonton stacked the line. They expected Montreal to rush the line of scrimmage to get the first down. But Etchevarry tricked the Eskimos with a pass over their heads. It fell into Patterson's hands for an easy touchdown.

Before the end of the first half, Edmonton scored the game's sixth touchdown. From the Montreal 15-yard line, Parker threw a short pass to Bob Heydenfeldt. The receiver caught the ball 10 yards downfield and ran into the end zone for a touchdown. Bob Dean kicked his third convert to make the score Montreal 19–18.

At halftime, some easterners started to say their prediction of a Montreal victory would come true. But the Eskimos stuck to their game plan of grinding it out along the ground.

Normie recalled when he plunged through the line on a fake hand-off, while Parker shot around the end. Normie was tackled on the play and the referee was ready to blow his whistle until Normie pointed to Parker. Parker still had the ball. His deceptiveness allowed him to run and pass freely.

The game eventually turned in favour of the Eskimos in the third quarter. Montreal's defense could not halt the Edmonton offense. Normie started by scoring a touchdown. Soon after, Edmonton moved the ball from its own 13-yard line to the Montreal 3-yard line. They used only one passing play and no less than 11 punishing ground plays. Then Bright ran into the Montreal end zone for the touchdown.

The Als still had a slight chance to win. It appeared they would score another touchdown when Etchevarry moved his team from the 17-yard line to Edmonton's 21-yard line. However, on the next play Parker stepped in front of Montreal's Jim Mills and intercepted an Etchevarry pass.

"That pass had touchdown written all

over it," said Rollie Miles. "But when Jackie took it I think it broke the Als heart."

Eskimos fans realized that Montreal would not come back to win. Edmonton's Bob Dean closed the scoring with a single point and a field goal.

The Eskimos won the game 34–19. They were now the two-time Grey Cup champions. They were the first western team to win back-to-back championships.

For Edmonton players and fans, "the yell of fluke that burned western ears for a solid year was jammed down the eastern throats," wrote the *Journal*.

"The Eskimos showed the east what the west had know all along — the Eskimos had the most crushing, devastating, and vicious ground attacks ever put together in Canadian football," wrote the *Journal*.

Normie and Parker were at the centre of the ground attack. Normie was always ready to run with the ball, even if

After the 1954 Grey Cup, football fans carried Normie off the field on their shoulders.

it meant he would be tackled to the ground. In the final, he rushed for a Grey Cup record 145 yards.

For his efforts, Normie was named a Western First Team All-Star. He was also awarded the Most Outstanding Canadian football player award.

His last honour of 1955 came as a surprise to most. It etched his achievements

Kwong And John Bright Roll Up Ground Attack

Normie made newspaper headlines.

into the Canadian sports record forever. That December, Normie was named the Canadian Press Male Athlete of the Year. He joined an elite group of athletes in Canada. It was one of the greatest honours a Chinese Canadian had ever been given.

Normie wasn't just a role model to the Chinese Canadian community. He was now a national sports star. Surprisingly, he was not overly excited about these honours. Football is a team sport and these awards only honour the individual. Normie would rather have his team win than achieve an individual record. His focus on team play gained him even more respect on the field.

14 The City of Champions

In 1956, Normie picked up where he left off during the 1955 season. He continued to be one of the most feared fullbacks in football. After nine league games he rushed for 819 yards. He was, again, the leading rusher in the league.

On October 15, Normie set a new rushing record while playing against the Blue Bombers. In that game, he rushed for 123 yards. He broke his own rushing record with two games left in the schedule.

By the end of the season, he had rushed for a new record of 1,437 yards.

The Eskimos did not have as successful a season. In 1955, the Eskimos were unbeatable. They encountered more competition in 1956. The league's talent was much more balanced. But they weren't strong enough to knock Edmonton out of top spot. They earned a bye into the western finals.

Unlike past western finals, the Eskimos would face the Saskatchewan Roughriders. The Roughriders surprised the Eskimos in the first game. They defeated the defending Grey Cup champs 23–22.

The Eskimos lost more than just the game. They also lost regular halfback Earl Lindley. He injured his shoulder.

Coach Pop Ivy was going to try the biggest gamble of his Canadian football coaching career. He moved Jackie Parker out of the quarterback position into the halfback slot. He then promoted backup quarterback Don Getty to the starting job.

Getty was a 22-year-old Canadian. He joined the Eskimos in 1955 and just watched from the bench. He played very little, and was not in the plans. There were no Canadian starting quarterbacks in the league. Now, he had the weight of a team and a city's dreams on his shoulders. Many supporters thought Pop was crazy, but the coach stood by his decision.

Nineteen thousand Edmonton fans showed up at Clarke Stadium to watch the second game of the western final. Many came to see if the experiment would work. They usually trusted the coach, but they thought this could be their last game of the season.

Everyone soon learned Getty was not hopeless at quarterback. A Canadian could guide a team to victory. He was at the helm for all three Eskimos touchdown drives. He topped it off by scoring one of those touchdowns himself.

The Eskimos won the second game 20–12. Coach Ivy instantly went from being crazy to being a genius.

Pop kept this lineup for the third game. A Clarke Stadium record crowd attended the game. The 22,461 fans came to cheer on the Eskimos to a third straight western championship.

Nothing could stop the Eskimos in the game. Not freezing weather, a 56-kilometre an hour wind, or, least of all, the Roughriders. The Eskimos humbled the Roughriders and won 51–7. It had been ten years since a Canadian quarterbacked a team to a western championship.

For the third year in a row, the Eskimos would face the Alouettes in the Grey Cup final. Montreal was, again, favoured to win. The game was back at Varsity Stadium in Toronto. Again, a western team would travel east. With them, they were taking the hopes and dreams of all western fans.

The critics expected Getty to collapse under the pressure of a final. They believed Canadian quarterbacks were not as good as Americans. That is why Getty was the first Canadian to start a Grey Cup since 1947.

Even though the Eskimos had a rookie quarterback they still had the split-t formation. The Als couldn't figure it out in their first two meetings. Pop had a hunch they would still have trouble with it.

Pop was right. Edmonton won their third straight Grey Cup. The final score was Edmonton 50, Montreal 27.

Normie was not a factor in the Grey Cup final. He was injured, so Getty turned to Johnny Bright for most of the inside running. But Normie still had a record-setting regular season. He was one of the reasons the Eskimos made it to the finals. These accomplishments were not forgotten when they handed out the year-end awards.

Norm was again named the Most Outstanding Canadian player, and named a Western First Team All-Star. He also placed second in voting for the Canadian Press Male Athlete of the Year.

The Eskimos and the Grey Cup

In 1921, the Eskimos became the first western Canadian team to play for the Grey Cup. They are the most successful Canadian Football League team over the past 60 years. They appeared in 22 Grey Cup finals. They won the big game 13 times: 1954–56, 1975, 1978–82, 1987, 1993, 2003, and 2005.

15 Endgame

When are you going to retire? That is the most common question asked of all veteran athletes. After the 1956 Grey Cup final, Normie was asked that very question. Reporters surrounded him and asked how much football did the China Clipper have left? At twenty-six, Normie was still a young player. He was only three years older than star Jackie Parker. But he had a veteran's worth of experience. Normie had been playing nearly ten years of pro football. He was a veteran and had the veteran reply.

"Another couple of years and I'll be happy," said Normie to the reporters.

Normie didn't want to play longer than he should. He played with veterans who should have retired before their bodies aged too much and their skills diminished. Normie wanted to retire at the top of his game. He didn't want to be remembered as the aged veteran.

Before the start of the 1957 season, the Eskimos played exhibition games in the United States. For many of the Americans the most interesting aspect of these games was Normie. One Chinese-American was quoted in a San Francisco newspaper saying, "the best thing about Canadian football was Normie Kwong."

Back in Canada, Normie gained a devoted following in the Chinese-Canadian community. During games people would

Normie was a hard player to bring down. Sometimes it took two players to accomplish the task.

gather around televisions at Chinese restaurants to watch Normie play. Children looked up to Normie. He gave them hope that they could do anything they wanted to do. There weren't many Chinese-Canadian role models as visible as Normie.

Norm's regular season rushing record was smashed by Johnny Bright in 1957. The Eskimos were still the strongest rushing team in Canada. At the heart of that success was the split-t formation. The formation made these two players legends of the game.

All great teams have to come to an end. The Eskimos were one of the strongest teams in Canadian football at the time. They looked like they were unbeatable. It seemed like they would win the Grey Cup every year. Eskimos fans expected it of their team. A 14–2 regular season record in 1957 made it look like it could happen again.

But the Eskimos faced their old rivals in the western final. The Blue Bombers were the toughest competition for the Eskimos in the past four seasons. Former Bombers player Bud Grant coached the team. In his rookie season as coach, he put together a strong squad. To match the rushing of Bright and Normie, the Bombers had Gerry James and Leo Lewis. At quarterback

Parker, Kwong Score Touchdowns For Eskimos In Battle Of Lines

they had rookie Kenny Ploen, whose talents were just being realized.

In the 1957 western final, Edmonton tried to live up to their reputation. They were the heavy favourites to win in straight games. But the Alouettes were the favourites once, too, and look what the Eskimos did to them.

The first game was played in Winnipeg. Winnipeg Stadium held over 20,000 fans, but only 13,000 showed up for the first game. They didn't think their team would win, so they didn't come out to support them. The big, bold Bombers wanted the game more than the Eskimos. They won 19–7.

In Edmonton, 18,500 fans felt the last-minute excitement of a Jackie Parker miracle. In the final second of the second game, he scored the points needed for an Eskimos victory. Edmonton won 5–4.

The Eskimos' hopes for a fourth straight Grey Cup were dashed in the final game. Winnipeg won 17–2 and were crowned western champs. Grit, pride, and desire were what won it for the Bombers.

The Eskimos were never the same after that loss.

Before the start of the 1958 season, Eskimos fans had a series of shocks. Pop Ivy announced he was going to coach the Chicago Cardinals of the NFL. At

Birth of the CFL

The Canadian Football League was formed in 1958. The CFL was solely a professional football league. It was split into eastern and western divisions. It wasn't until 1961 that the two divisions played each other during the regular season.

the same time, it was rumoured Parker would be joining the NFL. He eventually announced he was staying in Edmonton.

During the 1958 season, Normie hinted at retirement. His off-field focus had turned to Vancouver. He was getting into the commercial real estate business. He also had a girlfriend, Mary Lee.

Normie requested a trade in 1959 to the B.C. Lions. He wanted to be closer to his business and his girlfriend. The two teams couldn't come to an agreement. Normie then refused to sign with the Eskimos. It looked like he was going to retire. But after missing the first 23 days of training camp, he returned to the roster.

The same scenario played out before the 1960 season. Normie decided to retire after failing to reach a contract agreement with the Eskimos. He also married his girlfriend. He decided to start his life after football.

"I hate to quit playing, as I love the

Kwong Will Set Record
If Opportunity Knocks

game, but I don't think I'll be changing my mind this time," said Normie, who held the all-time rushing record for Canadian football with 8,257 yards.

One month later, Normie changed his mind. At 30 years of age, he was going to play one more season. Teammates and a contract offer he could not refuse brought him back to football.

Normie's football career ended like it began. He played in the 1960 Grey Cup final. The Eskimos' opponents were the Ottawa Rough Riders. They played at Empire Stadium in Vancouver.

The Eskimos' stars had aged. Players like Normie, Johnny Bright, Jackie Parker, and Rollie Miles were all older players.

They were up against a younger, bigger team. Edmonton proved to be no match for the easterners. Ottawa defeated the Eskimos 16–6.

Normie's dream of playing pro football had been played out over 13 seasons, seven Grey Cup finals, and four Grey Cup wins. His only regret, he said, was that his departure from pro football was not on the same happy note that marked his entry.

After the 1960 season, he finally retired. His body was telling him it was the end.

"The pressure of trying to get out there every game and live up to the past gets to be so tough now, that it's not worth it anymore," said Normie.

When Normie retired, he held over 30 Canadian Football League records. A lot of the records were broken over time, but the image of Norm being one of the game's greatest rushers would never be broken. He was the leader in the development of modern football. His achievements became the landmarks of a great career. No matter what he was doing, he would always be the China Clipper, sailing through to achieve great things.

The Original China Clipper

Hockey player Larry Kwong was the first Chinese Canadian to play in the NHL. He played one game for the New York Rangers in 1948. He played senior and professional hockey from 1939 to 1958. He later became a tennis coach. His nicknames were China Clipper and King Kwong. He is no relation to Norm Kwong.

Epilogue

Calgary fans never let the Stampeders forget the day they traded away Normie. His career was not done when he left Calgary. It was just getting started. He was not just a hometown boy playing pro football. He became one of the greatest rushers in Canadian football history.

Before the start of the 1956 football season, the Calgary Booster Club honoured Normie. Six hundred people came out to a celebration dinner. It was called "Kwong fest."

Normie heard tributes from various people he met during his career. Four of his pro-football coaches described their experiences with the Calgary-born football star. During all the speeches, Normie's father, Charles Kwong, sat beside his son. He felt great pride for the way his fellow Calgarians honoured his son.

Les Lear, Normie's first pro coach, said, "the rookie had the burning desire to go on to become a great football player," and after a season sitting on the bench Lear gave him that chance.

Annis Stukas, former Eskimos coach, talked about obtaining Normie for Edmonton in 1950.

"I watched him play against us the previous year and that was enough for me, I wasn't sure what we were going to do with him, but I wanted to make certain he didn't play against us," said Stukas.

The most surprising speaker was Reg Clarkson. He was the player Calgary traded for Norm.

"Kwong isn't good all the time," said Clarkson, "but when he isn't good, he's terrific."

Gordie Hunter summed it up best in his newspaper column the next day.

He wrote, "I guess Normie Kwong qualifies as just about the most successful success story you could want to find. A local boy who made good at home and then moved on to Edmonton, overcoming what medics said was a permanent ankle injury and went on to be known far and wide as the best fullback in Canadian football."

After retiring from football, Normie's life centred on his family and his various business ventures. He became very successful in commercial real estate. He and his wife Mary raised four boys: Gregory, Bradley, Martin, and Randall.

Normie's football achievements were celebrated over the years. He was inducted into the Canadian Sports Hall of Fame, Canadian Football Hall of Fame, Alberta Sports Hall of Fame, and Eskimos Wall of Fame. He was also made a member of the Order of Canada.

Normie returned to the world of sports in 1980. He became one of the original owners of the Calgary Flames.

The Flames won the Stanley Cup in 1989. Normie was one of two people to win both a Grey Cup and a Stanley Cup. His Stanley Cup ring is one of his most cherished possessions. He remained a team owner until 1994.

Normie became involved with the Stampeders again in 1988. By the mid-1980s the team had financial difficulties. They were not doing well on the field either. They were on the verge of folding. Normie became the team's president and general manager. He helped them become profitable again. He put together a great team that made fans excited about the Stamps again. By the time he left in 1991, they were Grey Cup contenders.

Normie's life took an unexpected turn one day in 2005. He received a phone call from Paul Martin, the Prime Minister of Canada. At first Normie didn't believe it was Paul Martin. He thought somebody was playing a trick on him. But once he believed it was the Prime Minister, he received a great shock. Paul Martin asked Normie if he would like to be the next Lieutenant-Governor of Alberta. Without hesitation he accepted his new job. It was one of the greatest honours given to a citizen of Alberta.

On January 20, 2005, Normie was sworn in as Alberta's sixteenth Lieutenant-Governor. His term of office lasted five years.

In sport he was called the China Clipper. As Lieutenant-Governor he took on a new title: the Honourable Norman Kwong. He would keep that title for the rest of his life.

"They talk a lot about the American Dream. Well, my story has to be the Canadian Dream," said Normie. "My father was an immigrant grocer who couldn't even vote in Canada until his fortieth year in Canada and he has a son who became the Lieutenant-Governor of this province. There are not many places where you can achieve that kind of success."

Normie achieved in life what most people only dream about doing. Nothing was handed to him though. A desire to succeed propelled him through life. On the way he became a football legend, a successful business man, a loving family man, and a respected member of society. Not bad for the son of a Chinese immigrant who started playing football on the vacant lots of Calgary.

Football Basics

Football is a game of speed, strength, and strategy. The offense tries to move the ball forward on the field, while the defense tries to stop them. The action is not continuous. After each play, the referee blows the whistle, and the offense and defense set up again on opposite sides of the line of scrimmage.

The offense has three downs (chances) to advance the ball ten yards and earn a first down. (In football measurements are in yards not metres. A yard is the same length as a metre.) Moving the ball forward involves either running or passing. When the offense crosses the goal line and enters the end zone, they score a touchdown, worth six points. After a touchdown, the scoring team attempts a kick. One player holds the ball on its end while the kicker tries to boot it through the uprights, which are football's goalposts. The kick is called an extra point or a convert, and adds a single point to the total score.

When the offense lines up for a play, there is normally an offensive line in front, a few receivers arranged on either side of the offensive line, and a backfield (including the quarterback and other backs) in behind.

Players on the offensive line are usually big and strong. They protect the backfield players, so they can make plays. The offensive line is made up of ends, tackles, and a centre who snaps the ball back to the quarterback.

Once the quarterback has the ball, he

can keep it and run himself (known as a quarterback sneak). He may also hand off the ball to one of the running backs (a fullback, or a halfback), who can carry the ball forward. Or he may attempt a pass and throw the ball through the air. If the pass is caught before the ball touches the ground, it is referred to as a reception, or a completion.

The defense, meanwhile, tries to tackle the offensive players to the ground before they advance down the field. On passing plays, the defense tries to make an interception by catching the ball thrown by the quarterback before it reaches its target. The players making interceptions are usually the defensive backs.

If the offense is close enough to the end zone, they may kick a field goal, rather than running with, or passing, the ball. Much like a convert, a field goal involves kicking the ball through the opposing team's uprights. A field goal earns a team three points.

When the offense keeps the ball moving forward on a series of plays, they are on a drive. If they score or give up the ball, the drive ends and the other team begins their drive.

As in most sports, the team with the most points at the end of the game wins.

Glossary

Ball carrier: Any player carrying the ball and attempting to advance it on the ground.

Blocking: When a player obstructs another player with his body.

Defense: The players that are responsible for keeping the opposition out of their end zone.

Defensive line: The defensive players who line up on the line of scrimmage opposite the offensive linemen. A team's first line of defense.

Down: One of three chances a team on offense has to gain ten yards.

Drive: The series of plays a team puts together in an attempt to score.

End zone: The area at each end of the field that a team tries to enter to score a touchdown.

First down: The first play of every series. The offense must gain ten yards or more in three downs to be awarded another first down.

Halfback: An offensive player who carries the ball on running plays. Also known as a running back.

Line of scrimmage: An imaginary line stretching the width of the field that separates the two teams prior to the snap of the ball.

Major: Another term for touchdown.

Offense: The team that has possession of the football and attempts to advance it toward the defense's goal line.

Offensive line: The five offensive players that line up on the line of scrimmage and block for the quarterback and ball carriers.

Open up holes: Pushing the opposition aside to make room in their defense for a ball carrier to run with the ball.

Point after touchdown: After a touchdown, the scoring team is allowed to add another point by kicking the football through the uprights of the goalpost.

Possession: To be holding or in control of the football.

Receiver: An offensive player who catches or attempts to catch a forward pass.

Running back: An offensive player who runs with the football. Also known as the halfback or fullback.

Running play: A play where the offense tries to advance the ball by running with it.

Rush: To run from the line of scrimmage with the football.

Tackling: Contacting a ball carrier to

cause him to touch the ground with any part of his body except his hands, which ends the play.

Touchdown: When a team crosses the opponent's goal line with the ball, catches a pass in the opponent's end zone, or recovers a loose ball in the opponent's end zone.

Yard: A unit of measurement equal to three feet or one meter.

Yardage: The amount of yards gained or lost during a play, game, or career.

Yard line: A marking on the field that indicates the distance in yards to the nearest goal line.

Acknowledgements

This story became another Recordbooks account of a fading piece of Canadian sports history. That makes the hunt for information a little bit tougher. The research took me through many different forms of media and car trips across Canada.

I would like to first thank the Honourable Norm Kwong, his wife Mary, and the office of Alberta's Lieutenant-Governor for their time for an interview. It was an experience I will not forget.

My research started by searching through various newspaper archives including the *Edmonton Journal*, *Calgary Herald*, *Winnipeg Free Press*, *Vancouver Sun*, *Toronto Star*, and *Globe and Mail*. I was not alive during the playing years of Norm, so I didn't have a feel for that time in football. To gain that knowledge I read various books on Canadian football history including *100*

Years of Canadian Football by Gordon Currie, *The Grey Cup Story* by Jack Sullivan, *Canadian Football: The Grey Cup Years* by Frank Cosentino, *Legends of Autumn* by Dennis Boyd, and *Greatest Grey Cups* by Graham Kelly.

The Internet is becoming an increasingly important source of information. I was able to watch and listen to various interviews with Norm.

Off the page, I would like to thank the people who supported me during the writing of this book. Like every book, it comes down to four people — my parents, my wife Shelley, and my editor Carrie Gleason. Thank you all.

Most importantly I would like to thank publisher James Lorimer for his continued support of the series. It is the only series focusing on Canadian sports history. This country has an exciting history and this series filled the void to bring it back to life.

About the Author

Richard Brignall is a journalist from Kenora, Ontario. He is a graduate of the University of Manitoba and former managing editor of its student newspaper, *the Manitoban*. He has written articles for *Cottage Life* and *Outdoor Canada*. He was previously a sports reporter for the *Kenora Daily Miner and News*. He is the author of several books in the Recordbooks series.

Photo Credits

We gratefully acknowledge the following sources for permission to reproduce the images in this book:

City of Edmonton Archives: p 23, p 62, p 66, p 82, p 96, p 113, p 123.

Courtesy of the *Edmonton Journal*: p 90, p 114, p 125, p 128.

Glenbow Archives ND-3-7050b: p 18, cover (top).

The Canadian Football Hall of Fame and Museum: p 76, cover.

Index

A

Abbruzzi, Pat, 109

Act to Restrict and
  Regulate Chinese
  Immigrants, 15

Anderson, Sugarfoot, 46

Aquirre, Joe, 65

Arnold, Claude, 64, 65,
  72, 79, 80

awards, 25, 60, 83, 113,
  114, 120, 131, 134

B

Battle of Alberta, 56

Bright, Johnny, 78, 99,
  100, 101, 102, 109, 111,
  119, 123, 124, 128

C

Canadian Football
  League, 126

captaincy, 83

Chambers, Jumbo, 65

Charter of Human
  Rights, 19

childhood, 17-8

Chinese Exclusion Act,
  16, 19

Chinese Immigrant Act, 16

Chinese name, 19

Clarke Stadium, 69, 117,
  118

Clarkson, Reg, 58, 59,
  132, 133

D

De Marco, Mario, 71

Dean, Bob, 88, 94, 110,
  112

double-fullback
  formation, 99, 100, 101

Douglas, Glen, 46

E

Empire Stadium, 108, 128

Etchevarry, Sam "The
  Rifle", 86, 88, 89, 108,
  109, 110, 111

F

Faloney, Bernie, 79, 80,
  81, 82, 88, 89, 98

Filchock, Frankie, 45-6,
  47, 57, 64, 67, 68, 73

G

general manager, 134

Getty, Don, 117, 118,
  119

Grant, Bud, 124

H

Head Tax, 15, 16, 17
Hewitt, Foster, 97
Heydenfeldt, Bob, 110
Hill, Norm, 40, 46
Hunsinger, Chuck, 89, 92
Hunter, Gordie, 133

I

immigration, 14, 15, 16, 17
Ivy, Frank "Pop", 77, 78,
  79, 80, 84, 98, 99, 101,
  104, 116, 117, 118, 119,
  126

J

James, Gerry, 102, 103,
  104, 124

K

Keys, Eagle, 95
King, Mike, 57
Kwong, Charles Lim, 17,
  18, 132
Kwong, Lilly (nee Lee),
  17, 18, 22, 23, 24, 25,
  49
Kwong, Mary (nee Lee),
  127, 133

L

Lear, Les, 27, 28, 29, 30,
  31, 36, 38, 40, 41, 42,
  46, 48, 132
Lewis, Leo, 124
Lieutenant-Governor of
  Alberta, 135, 136
Lindley, Earl, 88, 99, 102,
  116
Lippmann, Glenn, 91

M

McCallum, Hiram, 11, 12
McKay, Don, 10
Mewata Stadium, 30, 33
Miles, Rollie, 57, 65, 78,
  80, 81, 88, 99, 101, 102,
  112, 128
Mills, Jim, 109, 111
Morganson, Bunny, 87
Morris, Frank, 69

N

National Football League
  (NFL), 27, 46, 51, 63,
  77
nicknames, 44, 82, 130
North Hill Blizzards, 24,
  25

O

O'Quinn, Red, 86, 88,
  89

P

Pantages, Rod, 43, 44, 47

Parker, Jackie, 78, 79, 80, 81, 82, 92, 93, 94, 98, 101, 102, 108, 109, 110, 111, 112, 116, 121, 125, 127, 128

Patterson, Hal, 86, 109, 110

Ploen, Kenny, 125

Poole, Ray, 92

Prather, Rollie, 67, 68, 71, 92

R

Royal York Hotel, 11, 12, 39

Royal, Darrell, 73, 74, 75, 77

S

Spaith, Keith, 43, 46

split-t formation, 74, 75, 76, 77, 124

statistics, 53, 60, 84, 94, 99, 102, 103, 106, 113, 115, 116, 128, 129

Strode, Woody, 43

Stukas, Annis, 57, 132

T

t-formation, 74

Trawick, Herb, 46, 88, 92

V

Varsity Stadium, 37, 45, 118

voting, 19

W

wages, 28, 40

Wagner, Virgil, 47

Wilkinson, Bud, 73, 77

Winnipeg Stadium, 125

Wirkowski, Nobby, 71

Wright, Howard, 102

More gripping underdog tales of
sheer determination and talent!